The New Novello Choral Edition

JOHANN SEBASTIAN BACH

Magnificat in D (BWV243)

for solo voices, SATB chorus and orchestra

Vocal score

Edited by Neil Jenkins

Order No: NOV079024

NOVELLO PUBLISHING LIMITED
14 - 15 Berners Street, London W1T 3LJ

It is requested that on all concert notices and programmes acknowledgement is made to 'The New Novello Choral Edition'.

Es wird gebeten, auf sämtlichen Konzertankündigungen und Programmen 'The New Novello Choral Edition' als Quelle zu erwähnen.

Il est exigé que toutes notices et programmes de concerts, comportent des remerciements à 'The New Novello Choral Edition'.

Orchestral material is available on hire from the Publisher.

Orchestermaterial ist beim Verlag erhältlich.

Les partitions d'orchestre sont en location disponibles chez l'editeur.

Permission to reproduce the Preface of this Edition must be obtained from the Publisher.

Die Erlaubnis, das Vorwort dieser Ausgabe oder Teile desselben zu reproduzieren, muß beim Verlag eingeholt werden.

Le droit de reproduction de ce document à partir de la préface doit être obtenu de l'éditeur.

Cover illustration: facsimile of the first page of the original score of Bach's *Magnificat* in D. Reproduced by permission of the Berlin State Library (Music Department with Mendelssohn Archive) [Mus. ms. Bach P39, 1. Notenseite]

© 2008 Novello & Company Limited

Published in Great Britain by Novello Publishing Limited
Head office: 14 - 15 Berners Street, London W1T 3LJ
Tel +44 (0)207 612 7400   Fax +44 (0)207 612 7545

Sales and Hire: Music Sales Distribution Centre
Newmarket Road, Bury St Edmunds, Suffolk, IP33 3YB
Tel +44 (0)1284 702600   Fax +44 (0)1284 768301

Web: www.musicroom.com   www.chesternovello.com

CONTENTS

PREFACE

Magnificat in D (BWV243) has long been regarded as one of Bach's finest short choral works and is frequently performed on festive occasions. It is based on an earlier Magnificat setting in E flat (BWV243a) dating from 1723, Bach's first year as Kantor at the Thomaskirche in Leipzig. According to Robert L. Marshall, Bach had the luxury of almost six weeks in which to prepare BWV243a, a setting of the Sanctus (BWV238) and revisions to Cantata BWV63 all for performance on Christmas Day 1723[1]. This earlier E flat setting of the Magnificat has twelve movements plus an additional four Christmas Lauds (interspersed between the Magnificat movements), and provided Bach with an early opportunity to impress his new employers and congregation with a work double the length of his normal weekly cantatas.

The structure and tonal scheme shared by both versions of the Magnificat are satisfyingly symmetrical and have long been admired by scholars. The choruses are followed by three groups of solo movements in related keys, the last of which is always for an increased number of singers (thus No. 3 is a solo, No. 6 is a duet and No. 10 is a trio). So as to break up an otherwise long sequence of arias, the chorus returns in No. 4 to sing two appropriate words detached from the previous aria: 'omnes generationes' (all generations'). C.S. Terry noted that a similar device had been used in a Magnificat in G minor attributed to Albinoni[2]. Bach used this simple idea to craft twenty-seven bars of majestic counterpoint leading to a splendid climax on a dominant minor ninth chord at bar 24 (left unresolved in the earlier version). No. 10 employs the tonus peregrinus, to which the Magnificat was traditionally chanted, as an instrumental counterpoint to the voices: in the first version this is given to a solo trumpet, and in the revision to unison oboes.

In No. 11 ('Sicut locutus est') a reference to 'our forefathers, Abraham and his seed' inspired Bach to look back at the music of his predecessors in Leipzig, such as Johann Kuhnau (1660-1722), and the music of this movement is written in an old-fashioned a cappella fugal style that would have been familiar to earlier congregations. The lesser doxology 'Gloria Patri et filio' reaffirms the work in its home key, and at the words 'sicut erat in principio' ('as it was at the beginning') Bach reintroduces the music of the work's opening bars. Although this device was not unknown to composers of the Baroque, its appropriateness at this point would have appealed to Bach. The composition is full of such delightful word painting: 'dispersit' is vigorously scattered; 'exaltavit' and 'deposuit' graphically depict 'rising' and 'falling'; and, in the closing bars of No. 6, the words 'timentibus eum' ('them that fear him') are sung to a plangent repeated note (particularly at bar 31) which suggests intensely controlled nervousness.

Bach's revision of his Magnificat in E flat to form the Magnificat in D took place sometime between 1728 and 1733 (possibly 1735)[3] and the new work was probably premiered on 2nd July 1733[4], when the Feast of the Visitation of Mary coincided with the end of national mourning for the death of the Elector of Saxony, Friedrich August I.

The three most obvious differences between the two versions are: the removal of the four Christmas Lauds; the downward transposition into D major, which was a better key for the trumpets and drums and frequently used for such festal music (cf. movements in the Christmas Oratorio and B Minor Mass) and the augmentation of the orchestra by the introduction of a pair of flutes throughout (BWV243a only calls for two recorders or flauti dolci in movement No.9).

Removing the Christmas Lauds consolidated the Magnificat in D as a work that could be used on those high feasts (some fifteen in the Lutheran Church) when an elaborate setting of the Latin Magnificat was permitted.

In addition to minor revisions to the music text, Bach also made changes to the scoring, most notably in No. 10. This movement has its obbligato scored for oboes rather than solo trumpet. This alteration may have been due to the fact that Bach's favourite trumpeter (Gottfried Reiche, 1667-1734) was no longer available, and it could not be entrusted to any other player.

1   R.L. Marshall: *On the origin of the Magnificat, The Music of Johann Sebastian Bach* (New York: Schirmer, 1989)

2   C.S. Terry: *Bach: The Magnificat, Lutheran Masses and Motets* (London, 1929).

3   M. Boyd: 'Bach', J.M. Dent *The Master Musicians* (London, 1983).

4   S Heighes: 'Magnificat' in *J.S. Bach: Oxford Composer Companions* ed. M. Boyd (Oxford, 1999).

Magnificat in D was revived by C.P.E. Bach for a performance in 1786 when he succeeded Telemann as director of music at the five principal churches in Hamburg.

EDITORIAL PROCEDURE

Text

The Latin text is the standard version of the Magnificat (taken from Luke i, 46-55) found in the Vulgate bible. Bach's only deviation from this text is his omission of the word 'eius' in the line 'Et misericordia eius a progenie in progenies timentibus eum' (No. 6) rendering its meaning as 'And [his] mercy is on them that fear him'. The fact that C.P.E. Bach and Schütz use the complete sentence in their Magnificat settings seems to indicate that this was an oversight by Bach, rather than a customary change made in Lutheran worship.

Music

The music of this edition was derived from the Neuen Bach-Ausgabe (1955/59). Simrock and Bachgesellschaft edition of BWV243 [11. Band, Teil 1] were also consulted. Editorial dynamics, instructions and ornaments are shown in square brackets, editorial ties and slurs are shown as 'cut' ties and 'cut' slurs (that is with a stroke through). The editorial continuo realisation is shown in small-sized notes.

Dynamics

Bach used dynamics sparingly in BWV243, sometimes using them to indicate the difference between an orchestral ritornello and an accompanying passage. A limited number of editorial dynamics have been added to the present edition.

Appoggiaturas

Editorial appoggiaturas have been added where they are missing from a passage when repeated.

THE REHEARSAL
PIANO ACCOMPANIMENT

I have provided a new rehearsal accompaniment, in which the material based on instrumental parts is in full-sized type and editorial realisation shown cue-sized. I have tried to represent all of the orchestration, although it has not been possible to preserve every part at the correct pitch.

THE ORCHESTRAL SCORE AND PARTS

The score and parts, available on hire from the publisher, are newly engraved and correspond exactly with this vocal score. The orchestral parts may be used for either period or modern instrument performances. A newly-realised Keyboard Continuo part is suitable for chamber organ or harpsichord.

The orchestration of the *Magnificat* in D is 2 flutes, 2 oboes, 3 trumpets, timpani and strings.

Oboes Bach's requirements were for two players doubling oboe and oboe d'amore. Transpositions of the d'amore music (Nos. 3 & 4) are given in an appendix to the part, this allowing the whole piece to be played on two oboes.

Trumpets and Timpani Three virtuoso players are required, with Trumpet 1 needing to reach d'''. The timpani are tuned to D and A.

Strings The string parts contain all the bowing and articulation found in the MS.

Keyboard Continuo

This is the part from which the continuo should be played. The vocal score is no adequate substitute since it is a piano reduction for rehearsal purposes. The keyboard continuo part contains the few continuo figures found in the MS.

ACKNOWLEDGEMENTS

Thanks are due to Hywel Davies for his help in seeing this edition through to publication.

Neil Jenkins

NOTE

The Novello edition of *Magnificat* in D (NOV070033), which this edition supersedes, was published in 1874 with an English translation by the Reverend John Troutbeck (1832-99), loosely based on the text found in The Book of Common Prayer. In the present edition the only English translations provided are those for the Christmas Lauds. The present edition of the *Magnificat* in D follows the layout of NOV070033 (except for page 36) to allow the two editions to be used side-by-side.

MAGNIFICAT in D

1 **[CHORUS]**

[Tpts., Timp., Fls., Obs., Stgs., Cont. Org.]

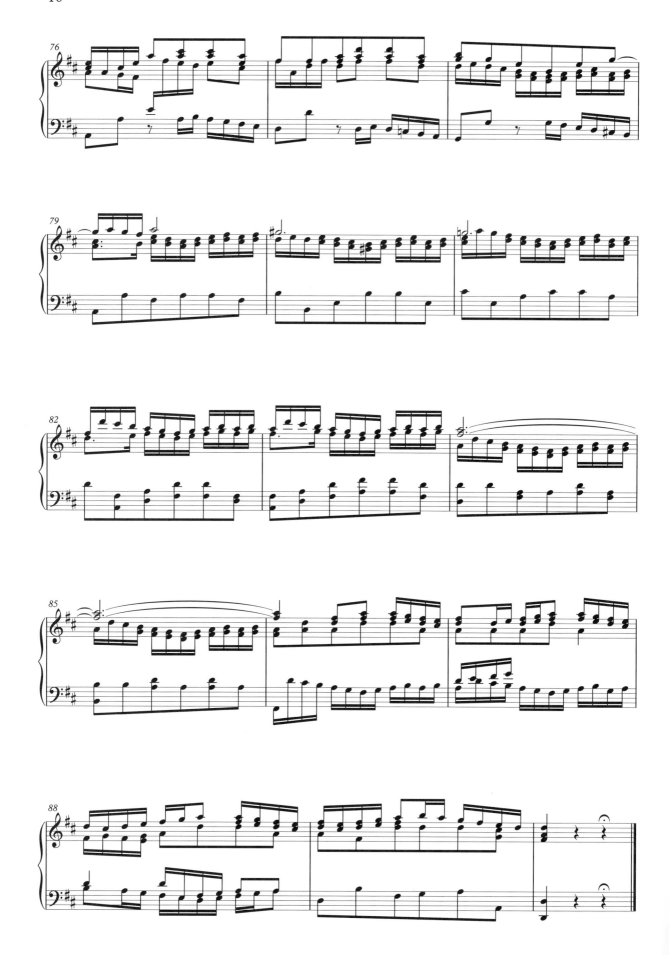

2 **[ARIA]**

SOPRANO 2 SOLO

Et ex - sul - ta - vit spi - ri - tus_ me - us,

Et ex - sul - ta - vit spi - ri - tus_ me - us,

3 **[ARIA]**

4 **[CHORUS]**

5 **[ARIA]**

[Cont. Org.]

BASS SOLO

Qui - a fe - cit__ mi - hi mag - na,

6 **[DUET]**

ALTO SOLO [*p*]

Et mi-se - ri-cor - di-a,_____ mi-se - ri - cor - di-a_____ a pro- ge -

TENOR SOLO [*p*]

Et mi-se - ri-cor - di-a,_____ mi-se - ri - cor - di-a_____ a pro- ge-ni-e

- ni - e in_____ pro-ge - ni - es;

in_ pro-ge-ni - es, in_ pro-ge - ni - es;

e - um, ti - men - ti-bus, ti - men - - - ti-bus, ti-

e - um, ti - men - ti-bus, ti - men - - - ti-bus, ti-

-men-ti-bus e - um, ti - men - - - ti-bus e - um.

-men-ti-bus e - um, ti - men - - - ti-bus e - um.

[*mf*]

(*p*)

7 [CHORUS]

8 **[ARIA]**

[Vlns.,
Cont. Org.]

TENOR SOLO

De - po - - - su - it, de -

et ex-al-ta - - - -

- vit hu - mi - les.

9 **[ARIA]**

[Fls., Cont. Org.]

ALTO SOLO

E - su - ri - en - tes im - ple - vit bo - nis,

e - su - ri - en - tes im - ple - vit bo - nis et di - vi - tes_ di - mi - sit, et

10 [TRIO]

46

11 **[CHORUS]**

12 **[CHORUS]**